Glances of World History

nuvisity

Published by nuvisity, 2024.

While every precaution has been taken in the preparation of this book, the publisher assumes no responsibility for errors or omissions, or for damages resulting from the use of the information contained herein.

GLANCES OF WORLD HISTORY

First edition. January 30, 2024.

Copyright © 2024 nuvisity.

ISBN: 979-8224046539

Written by nuvisity.

Contents

Chapter 1

Ancient Civilizations

The term "Ancient Civilizations" refers to the early, complex human societies that emerged and flourished in various parts of the world before the middle ages. These civilizations were characterized by advanced cultural, social, political, and technological achievements. These civilizations laid the groundwork for the development of human culture, technology, governance, and societal structures. Each of these societies had its unique features, but they shared common traits such as the development of agriculture, establishment of cities, creation of complex social structures, and formation of organized governments. Let's delve into key aspects of Ancient Civilizations.

1. **Sumerians (3200–2000 BCE):**

Geography and Society: Located in the southern part of Mesopotamia (present-day Iraq), the Sumerians were among the earliest known civilizations. They lived in independent city-states like Ur, Uruk, and Lagash.

Contributions:

The Sumerians are credited with inventing one of the earliest writing systems known as cuneiform, which involved wedge-shaped impressions on clay tablets.

Advanced irrigation techniques allowed for successful agriculture in a region with unpredictable river flooding.

The development of city-states like Ur and Uruk with ziggurats (stepped pyramids) as prominent architectural features.

2. **Ancient Egypt (3100–30 BCE):**

Geographical Location: Centered around the Nile River in Northeast Africa. Ancient Egypt emerged along the Nile River, allowing for fertile land and reliable agricultural practices. The river also served as a unifying force.

Contributions:

Pyramids and Pharaohs: The Egyptians are renowned for their monumental pyramids built as tombs for pharaohs, showcasing advanced architectural and engineering skills. The pharaohs were considered divine rulers with immense political and religious authority.

Hieroglyphic Writing: The Egyptians developed a complex writing system known as hieroglyphs, which was used for religious texts, monumental inscriptions, and administrative purposes.

3. Indus Valley Civilization (3300–1300 BCE)

Geographical Location: Flourished in the valley of the Indus River in present-day Pakistan and northwest India.

Contributions:

Well-planned cities like Mohenjo-daro and Harappa with sophisticated drainage and sewage systems.

The Indus people engaged in extensive trade with Mesopotamia. Archaeological findings include standardized weights and seals suggesting a high level of administrative organization.

Indus script, an ancient writing system that remains undeciphered.

Decline: The reasons for the decline of the Indus Valley Civilization are not entirely clear but may involve environmental factors, such as changes in the course of the rivers.

4. Ancient China (2100–221 BCE)

Geographical Location: East Asia, along the Yellow River (Huang He) and Yangtze River. Ancient China had a series of dynasties, including the Xia, Shang, and Zhou. Dynastic rule was a recurring theme in Chinese history.

Contributions:

Invention of early forms of writing on oracle bones and the use of bronze for ritual vessels.

Philosophical teachings of Confucius and Laozi, shaping Chinese culture and governance.

Construction of the Great Wall began during the Qin Dynasty to protect against invasions from nomadic tribes.

5. **Ancient Mesopotamia**:

Geographical Significance: Mesopotamia, located between the Tigris and Euphrates Rivers, was the cradle of civilization and home to several ancient cultures, including the Sumerians, Akkadians, Babylonians, and Assyrians.

Hammurabi's Code: The Babylonian king Hammurabi is famous for his law code, one of the earliest known sets of written laws, inscribed on a stele.

Epic of Gilgamesh: An epic poem from Mesopotamia, the Epic of Gilgamesh, is one of the earliest surviving works of literature.

These ancient civilizations laid the groundwork for future societies, influencing the development of human culture, technology, and governance. Their legacies continue to shape our understanding of the early stages of human civilization. Each had its unique characteristics, achievements, and challenges that contributed to the overall richness of the historical narrative.

Chapter 2

Classical Era

The "Classical Era" refers to a historical period that is often associated with the height of the classical civilizations of ancient Greece and Rome. This era is characterized by significant cultural, political, and intellectual achievements that laid the foundation for many aspects of Western civilization. The Classical Era typically spans from the 5th century BCE to the 4th century CE and is marked by distinct features in both Greek and Roman societies. Let's explore the key aspects of Classical Era.

1. **Ancient Greece (5th–4th centuries BCE)**

<u>Golden Age of Athens</u>: The 5th century BCE is often referred to as the Golden Age of Athens, marked by the leadership of statesmen like Pericles. This period saw the flourishing of democracy, philosophy, literature, and the arts.

<u>Philosophy</u>: Thinkers such as Socrates, Plato, and Aristotle made profound contributions to philosophy, exploring ethics, metaphysics, and political theory.

<u>Drama</u>: Playwrights like Aeschylus, Sophocles, and Euripides produced timeless tragedies and comedies. The Athenian amphitheater served as a venue for theatrical performances.

<u>Olympic Games</u>: The ancient Olympic Games, held every four years in Olympia, were a significant aspect of Greek culture, promoting athletic competition and pan-Hellenic unity.

Alexander the Great's Conquests (334–323 BCE)

<u>Macedonian Empire</u>: Under Alexander the Great, the Macedonian Empire expanded from Greece to Egypt, Persia, and into the Indian subcontinent.

<u>Hellenistic Period</u>: Following Alexander's death, his empire was divided among his generals, leading to the Hellenistic period. This era witnessed the spread of Greek culture and influence across a vast geographical area.

2. Roman Republic (509–27 BCE)

Roman Government: The Roman Republic was characterized by a system of checks and balances, with elected officials, the Senate, and popular assemblies. It gradually expanded its territory through military conquests.

Law and Governance: The development of Roman law, including the Twelve Tables, laid the groundwork for legal principles that influenced Western legal systems.

Punic Wars: Rome engaged in a series of wars with Carthage (Punic Wars), resulting in Roman dominance in the Mediterranean region.

Roman Empire (27 BCE–476 CE)

Pax Romana: The Roman Empire experienced a period of relative peace and stability known as the Pax Romana, lasting from the 1st century BCE to the 2nd century CE.

Engineering and Architecture: Romans were renowned for their engineering marvels, including the construction of aqueducts, roads, and the Colosseum.

Greco-Roman Culture: The blending of Greek and Roman cultures, often referred to as Greco-Roman or classical culture, influenced art, literature, and philosophy.

Decline of the Classical Era

External Pressures: The Classical Era faced challenges such as invasions by Germanic tribes, internal strife, and economic decline.

Transition to Late Antiquity: The Classical Era gradually transitioned into Late Antiquity, marked by the decline of the Western Roman Empire and the rise of new political and cultural entities.

The Classical Era had a profound impact on shaping the intellectual, political, and cultural landscape of Western civilization. The ideas and achievements of this period have left a lasting legacy that continues to influence modern thought and institutions.

Chapter 3

Ancient Religions

"Ancient Religions" refers to the diverse belief systems and spiritual practices that were prevalent in various civilizations during ancient times. These religions played a crucial role in shaping the cultures, societies, and worldviews of ancient people. Here's a more detailed exploration of this topic.

Ancient Mesopotamian Religion

Polytheism: Mesopotamian civilizations, including the Sumerians, Akkadians, Babylonians, and Assyrians, practiced polytheistic religions. They believed in a pantheon of deities governing different aspects of life.

Ziggurats: Temples called ziggurats were constructed as sacred structures, serving as the dwelling places for gods and goddesses.

Ancient Egyptian Religion

Polytheistic Pantheon: Like Mesopotamia, ancient Egypt had a polytheistic belief system with a diverse pantheon. Deities such as Ra, Osiris, and Isis held significant importance.

Afterlife: Egyptians believed in an afterlife and practiced elaborate funerary rituals, including mummification, to ensure a smooth transition to the next realm.

Ancient Indian Religions

Vedic Religion: In ancient India, the Vedic period (c. 1500–500 BCE) saw the development of the Vedic religion, which later evolved into Hinduism. The Rigveda is a key scripture from this period.

Brahmanism and Upanishads: The later Vedic period introduced Brahmanism, emphasizing ritualistic practices. The Upanishads, philosophical texts, explored the nature of reality and the self.

Ancient Chinese Religion

Ancestor Worship: Ancient Chinese religious practices often included ancestor worship, where respect and offerings were made to deceased ancestors.

Daoism and Confucianism: Daoism and Confucianism emerged as philosophical and ethical systems, influencing Chinese thought. Daoism emphasized harmony with the Dao (the Way), while Confucianism focused on ethical conduct and social harmony.

Ancient Greek Religion

Olympian Pantheon: Ancient Greece had a pantheon of gods and goddesses residing on Mount Olympus. Zeus, Hera, Athena, and Apollo were among the prominent deities.

Religious Rituals: Greeks engaged in various religious rituals, including sacrifices and festivals, to honor the gods. The Oracle at Delphi was a famous center for divination.

Ancient Roman Religion

Adoption of Greek Deities: Roman religion was heavily influenced by Greek mythology, with many deities being adapted and incorporated into the Roman pantheon.

State Religion: Romans practiced state-sponsored religious ceremonies, and the emperor held the title of Pontifex Maximus, the chief priest.

Ancient Judaic Religion

Monotheism: Ancient Judaism was one of the earliest monotheistic religions, emphasizing the worship of one God. Key religious texts include the Torah and the Ten Commandments.

Covenant with God: The concept of a covenant between God and the Israelites played a central role in Judaic beliefs.

Ancient Persian Religion (Zoroastrianism)

Zoroastrianism: Founded by the prophet Zoroaster, Zoroastrianism is one of the world's oldest known monotheistic religions. It introduced concepts like the struggle between good and evil and the final judgment.

These ancient religions provided frameworks for understanding the world, morality, and the divine. While some have evolved into contemporary faiths, others have faded into history, leaving behind a rich tapestry of mythologies, rituals, and moral teachings.

Chapter 4

Roman Empire

The Roman Empire was one of the most significant and enduring civilizations in ancient history, encompassing a vast territory and lasting for several centuries. It emerged from the Roman Republic and played a crucial role in shaping the political, cultural, and social foundations of Western civilization. The detailed exploration of the Roman Empire is covered in the succeeding paragraphs.

1. **<u>Formation and Expansion</u>**

Roman Republic The Roman Republic, established in 509 BCE after the overthrow of the Roman monarchy, was characterized by a system of checks and balances, with elected officials and a Senate.

Punic Wars Rome's expansion began with the Punic Wars against Carthage (264–146 BCE), resulting in Roman dominance in the western Mediterranean.

2. **<u>Transition to Empire</u>**

Julius Caesar In the 1st century BCE, political instability led to the rise of military commanders like Julius Caesar. His crossing of the Rubicon River in 49 BCE marked a pivotal moment, leading to the downfall of the Republic.

First Triumvirate and Civil Wars The First Triumvirate, consisting of Caesar, Pompey, and Crassus, eventually led to conflicts and civil wars, culminating in Caesar's victory at the Battle of Pharsalus in 48 BCE.

3. **<u>The Age of Augustus</u>**

Octavian (Augustus) Following Caesar's assassination in 44 BCE, his adopted son Octavian, later known as Augustus, became the first Roman Emperor. This marked the beginning of the Roman Empire in 27 BCE.

Pax Romana Augustus established a period of relative peace and stability known as the Pax Romana, lasting from 27 BCE to 180 CE. It facilitated economic prosperity and cultural flourishing.

4. Government and Administration

Imperial System The Roman Empire had an imperial system of governance, with emperors holding significant power. The Senate and various administrative officials played roles in governing provinces.

Roman Law The Romans developed a sophisticated legal system, with the Twelve Tables as a foundational legal code. The concept of "jus civile" (civil law) influenced later legal traditions.

5. Engineering and Architecture

Aqueducts and Roads Romans were renowned for their engineering achievements, constructing aqueducts to transport water and a vast network of roads for efficient communication and military movement.

Colosseum and Pantheon Iconic structures like the Colosseum and the Pantheon reflected Roman architectural prowess and served various functions, including entertainment and religious ceremonies.

6. Greco-Roman Culture

Blend of Cultures The Roman Empire absorbed and adapted elements of Greek culture, creating a Greco-Roman synthesis that influenced art, literature, philosophy, and architecture.

Latin Language Latin became the language of administration, and Roman literature, including works by Virgil and Cicero, contributed significantly to Western literature.

7. Challenges and Decline

Military Challenges The Roman Empire faced external threats from Germanic tribes, Parthians, and Sassanids. Internal strife and political instability further weakened the empire.

Economic Decline Economic challenges, including overreliance on slave labor and inflation, contributed to the decline of the Roman Empire.

8. Division and Fall

<u>Division into East and West</u> Diocletian divided the empire into the Eastern and Western Roman Empires in the 4th century CE to better manage governance.

<u>Fall of the Western Roman Empire (476 CE)</u> The Western Roman Empire faced continuous invasions, and in 476 CE, the last Roman emperor, Romulus Augustulus, was deposed by the Germanic chieftain Odoacer.

The Roman Empire's legacy is vast, influencing Western political systems, legal traditions, languages, and cultural practices. The fall of the Western Roman Empire marked the transition to the medieval period in European history.

Chapter 5

Medieval Period

The Medieval Period, also known as the Middle Ages, spanned roughly from the 5th to the late 15th century and represents a significant era in European history. It was characterized by a complex interplay of political, social, economic, and cultural developments. The Medieval Period is often divided into three sub-periods: the Early Middle Ages (c. 500–1000), the High Middle Ages (c. 1000–1300), and the Late Middle Ages (c. 1300–1500). Here's a detailed exploration of the Medieval Period:

1. **Early Middle Ages (c. 500–1000)**

Fall of the Western Roman Empire The period began with the decline and fall of the Western Roman Empire in 476 CE. This led to a power vacuum and the fragmentation of political authority.

Barbarian Invasions Germanic tribes, such as the Visigoths, Vandals, and Ostrogoths, invaded the former Roman territories, contributing to the disintegration of centralized governance.

Byzantine Empire While the Western Roman Empire declined, the Byzantine Empire in the East (with its capital at Constantinople) continued to thrive, preserving aspects of Roman culture and influencing neighboring regions.

2. **High Middle Ages (c. 1000–1300)**

Feudalism The feudal system emerged as a social, economic, and political structure. It involved a hierarchical arrangement of landownership, with kings, nobles, vassals, and peasants forming a complex network of relationships.

Manorialism Agricultural estates, known as manors, played a crucial role in the feudal economy. Peasants worked the land, and lords provided protection in exchange for labor and produce.

Rise of Towns and Trade Urbanization increased, and trade networks expanded. The growth of towns and the rise of merchant guilds contributed to economic development.

3. Late Middle Ages (c. 1300–1500)

Black Death The mid-14th century witnessed the devastating Black Death, a pandemic that significantly reduced the European population. Its impact had profound social, economic, and cultural consequences.

Hundred Years' War Fought between England and France from 1337 to 1453, the Hundred Years' War had a profound impact on military technology, tactics, and the development of nationalism.

Great Schism The Western Schism (1378–1417) divided the Catholic Church, with rival popes in Avignon and Rome. The Council of Constance eventually resolved the schism.

4. Intellectual and Cultural Developments

Scholasticism Scholastic philosophers sought to reconcile faith and reason, with figures like Thomas Aquinas making significant contributions.

Gothic Architecture The High and Late Middle Ages saw the rise of Gothic architecture, characterized by pointed arches, ribbed vaults, and flying buttresses in cathedral construction.

Medieval Literature Epic poems like "The Song of Roland" and Geoffrey Chaucer's "The Canterbury Tales" are notable literary works from this period.

5. Reconquista and Crusades

Reconquista In the Iberian Peninsula, Christian kingdoms gradually reclaimed territory from Islamic rule, a process known as the Reconquista.

Crusades A series of religiously motivated military expeditions were launched by European Christians to recapture Jerusalem and the Holy Land from Muslim control. The Crusades had political, economic, and cultural implications.

6. Decline and Transition

<u>Rise of Nation-States</u> Toward the end of the Middle Ages, the power of centralized monarchies increased, leading to the formation of early nation-states.

<u>Transition to the Renaissance</u> The Late Middle Ages set the stage for the Renaissance, characterized by a renewed interest in classical learning, art, and humanism.

The Medieval Period was a dynamic and transformative era that laid the groundwork for the subsequent developments in European history. While it faced challenges such as invasions, plagues, and political fragmentation, it also witnessed intellectual achievements, architectural marvels, and the emergence of distinctive cultural expressions.

Chapter 6

Islamic Golden Age

The Islamic Golden Age refers to a period of cultural, economic, scientific, and intellectual flourishing in the Islamic world, spanning roughly from the 8th to the 14th century. This era saw significant advancements in various fields, including science, medicine, mathematics, philosophy, literature, and architecture. The Islamic Golden Age was marked by a synthesis of knowledge from diverse cultures, including Greek, Roman, Persian, Indian, and Chinese influences. Here's a detailed exploration of the Islamic Golden Age.

1. Historical Context

Islamic Conquests Following the death of the Prophet Muhammad in 632 CE, the Islamic Caliphate rapidly expanded, conquering vast territories from Spain to India. The newly established Islamic Empire incorporated diverse cultures and civilizations.

Abbasid Caliphate The Abbasid dynasty, which came to power in 750 CE after overthrowing the Umayyads, played a crucial role in fostering the intellectual and cultural achievements of the Islamic Golden Age.

2. Advancements in Science and Mathematics

Translation Movement The House of Wisdom in Baghdad became a major center for the translation of Greek, Persian, and Indian texts into Arabic. Scholars translated works by Aristotle, Plato, Galen, Ptolemy, and others.

Mathematics Mathematicians like Muhammad al-Khwarizmi made significant contributions, introducing the concept of algebra and contributing to the development of trigonometry. The decimal system, including the use of Arabic numerals, spread to the Islamic world and later to Europe.

3. **Medicine and Healthcare**

Ibn Sina (Avicenna) Ibn Sina, a Persian polymath, wrote the "Canon of Medicine," a comprehensive medical encyclopedia that became a standard reference in both the Islamic and European worlds for centuries.

Advancements in Pharmacology Islamic scholars made significant contributions to pharmacology, studying and cataloging various medicinal plants and substances.

4. **Philosophy and Theology**

Philosophical Synthesis Islamic philosophers like Al-Farabi, Avicenna, and Averroes engaged in the study of philosophy and sought to reconcile Greek philosophy, especially the works of Aristotle, with Islamic theology.

The House of Wisdom Scholars in places like the House of Wisdom in Baghdad engaged in discussions on various philosophical and scientific topics, fostering an environment of intellectual exchange.

5. **Literature and Poetry**

The Thousand and One Nights This collection of Arabic folk tales, also known as "Arabian Nights," became widely known during the Islamic Golden Age, featuring stories like "Aladdin" and "Ali Baba."

Poetry Renowned poets like Omar Khayyam in Persia and Ibn al-Rumi in Andalusia made significant contributions to Arabic and Persian poetry.

6. **Architecture and Urban Development**

Islamic Architecture The Islamic Golden Age witnessed the construction of stunning mosques, palaces, and other architectural marvels. Notable examples include the Alhambra in Spain and the Great Mosque of Cordoba.

Urban Planning Cities like Baghdad, Cairo, and Cordoba were known for their advanced urban planning, featuring well-designed streets, markets, and public spaces.

7. Trade and Economic Prosperity

Trade Routes The Islamic Empire served as a bridge between East and West, facilitating trade along the Silk Road and connecting markets in Asia, Africa, and Europe.

Economic Prosperity Economic prosperity resulted from the expansion of trade, agricultural innovations, and a stable economic environment.

8. End of the Golden Age

Mongol Invasions The Mongol invasions, particularly the sack of Baghdad in 1258, dealt a severe blow to the intellectual and cultural achievements of the Islamic Golden Age. Many scholars fled to other regions.

The Islamic Golden Age left a lasting legacy, contributing to the Renaissance in Europe and influencing various fields of knowledge. While the period eventually gave way to political fragmentation and external pressures, its impact on the history of science, philosophy, and culture remains significant.

Chapter 7

<u>**Mongol Empire**</u>

The Mongol Empire was one of the largest and most influential empires in world history, spanning a vast territory across Eurasia during the 13th and 14th centuries. It was founded by Genghis Khan (c. 1162–1227), a Mongolian warrior and statesman, and later expanded under his successors. The Mongol Empire played a crucial role in connecting different cultures, facilitating trade and cultural exchange, and influencing the course of history. Here's a detailed exploration of the Mongol Empire.

1. <u>**Rise of Genghis Khan**</u>

<u>**Early Life**</u> Genghis Khan, originally named Temüjin, was born into a nomadic Mongol tribe in the early 12th century. He faced adversity, including the murder of his father, which led him to consolidate power and unite various Mongol tribes.

<u>**Unification of the Mongols**</u> Genghis Khan successfully united the disparate Mongol tribes through military conquests, strategic alliances, and political acumen.

2. <u>**Conquests and Military Strategies**</u>

<u>**Expansion**</u> Genghis Khan and his successors, including his sons and grandsons, led a series of military campaigns that resulted in the conquest of vast territories. The Mongols expanded into Central Asia, China, the Middle East, and Eastern Europe.

<u>**Military Tactics**</u> The Mongols were known for their innovative military tactics, including their skilled use of cavalry, mobility, and siege warfare. They adapted to different terrains and employed psychological warfare.

3. <u>**Administrative and Political System**</u>

<u>**Yassa**</u> Genghis Khan codified a set of laws known as the Yassa, which governed various aspects of Mongol life, including social order, military discipline, and trade.

Political Organization The Mongol Empire was divided into khanates, each ruled by a khan (leader) from Genghis Khan's family. Notable khanates included the Golden Horde, the Ilkhanate, the Chagatai Khanate, and the Yuan Dynasty.

4. Cultural and Religious Tolerance

Religious Freedom The Mongols were generally tolerant of various religions, allowing freedom of worship for their subjects. Religious institutions, such as churches and mosques, were often spared from destruction during conquests.

Cultural Exchange The Mongol Empire served as a conduit for cultural exchange between the East and West, fostering the transmission of ideas, technologies, and goods.

5. Pax Mongolica (Mongol Peace)

Trade and Commerce The Mongol Empire facilitated trade along the Silk Road, connecting Europe, the Middle East, and Asia. The resulting period of stability and security, known as Pax Mongolica, contributed to economic prosperity.

Cultural Interaction The movement of people and ideas during Pax Mongolica stimulated cultural and intellectual exchange between different regions.

6. Yuan Dynasty in China

Kublai Khan Genghis Khan's grandson, Kublai Khan, established the Yuan Dynasty in China in 1271. He became the first non-Chinese ruler to govern all of China.

Marco Polo The Venetian explorer Marco Polo visited the court of Kublai Khan and later wrote extensively about his experiences, contributing to European awareness of Asian cultures.

7. Decline and Legacy

Fragmentation After the death of Kublai Khan, the Mongol Empire gradually fragmented into smaller khanates, each ruled by different branches of the Mongol ruling family.

<u>End of the Empire</u> Internal conflicts, external invasions, and the decline of centralized authority contributed to the eventual disintegration of the Mongol Empire in the late 14th century.

The Mongol Empire had a profound impact on the world, shaping the course of history, facilitating cultural exchange, and leaving a lasting legacy in the regions it once controlled. While the empire itself did not endure, the memory of the Mongol conquests and their influence on global affairs persisted for centuries.

Chapter 8

<u>**Renaissance and Reformation**</u>

The Renaissance and Reformation were two interconnected movements that profoundly influenced the cultural, intellectual, religious, and social landscape of Europe during the late 14th to the 17th centuries. While the Renaissance marked a revival of classical learning and cultural achievements, the Reformation brought about significant changes in religious practices and doctrines. Here's a detailed exploration of both movements:

1. <u>**Renaissance (14th–17th centuries)**</u>

(a) <u>**Humanism and Revival of Classical Learning**</u>

<u>**Humanism**</u> The Renaissance was characterized by a humanistic approach, emphasizing the study of classical texts and a renewed interest in human potential and achievements.

<u>**Revival of Greek and Roman Literature**</u> Scholars like Petrarch and Erasmus played key roles in reviving classical literature, including works by Plato, Aristotle, and Cicero.

(b) <u>**Art and Architecture**</u>

<u>**Naturalism and Realism**</u> Renaissance artists, such as Leonardo da Vinci and Michelangelo, embraced naturalism and realism, moving away from medieval stylization.

<u>**Perspective in Art**</u> Innovations in perspective and techniques like chiaroscuro (use of light and shadow) were prominent in Renaissance art.

<u>**Architectural Achievements**</u> The era saw the construction of magnificent structures, including the Florence Cathedral and St. Peter's Basilica in Rome.

(c) <u>**Scientific Advancements**</u>

<u>**Observational Science**</u> Pioneering figures like Copernicus, Galileo, and Kepler challenged traditional views on astronomy and promoted a heliocentric model of the solar system.

Scientific Method The Renaissance laid the groundwork for the scientific method, emphasizing empirical observation, experimentation, and systematic inquiry.

(d) **Printing Press and Spread of Ideas**

Invention of the Printing Press Johannes Gutenberg's invention of the printing press around 1440 revolutionized the dissemination of knowledge and facilitated the spread of Renaissance ideas.

Impact on Education Books became more accessible, contributing to increased literacy rates and the democratization of knowledge.

2. **Reformation (16th century)**

(a) **Causes of the Reformation**

Corruption in the Church Widespread corruption, including the sale of indulgences, within the Catholic Church prompted calls for reform.

Humanist Criticism Humanist scholars like Erasmus criticized the Church's excesses and called for a return to the original teachings of Christianity.

(b) **Martin Luther and the 95 Theses (1517)**

Martin Luther A German monk, Martin Luther, posted his 95 Theses on the door of the Castle Church in Wittenberg, criticizing the sale of indulgences and questioning various Church practices.

Spread of Lutheranism Luther's ideas gained support, leading to the formation of the Lutheran Church and sparking the broader Protestant Reformation.

(c) **Spread of Protestantism**

Other Reformers Figures like John Calvin and Huldrych Zwingli led movements that resulted in the establishment of Calvinism and other Protestant denominations.

Impact on Religious Diversity The Reformation led to the fragmentation of Western Christianity, with the emergence of various Protestant denominations alongside the Catholic Church.

(d) **Council of Trent and Catholic Counter-Reformation**

<u>Council of Trent (1545–1563)</u> The Catholic Church responded to the Reformation with the Council of Trent, addressing issues of corruption, reaffirming doctrine, and initiating reforms.

<u>Formation of the Jesuits</u> The Society of Jesus, or Jesuits, founded by Ignatius of Loyola, played a key role in promoting Catholic education and missionary activities.

(e) **<u>Political and Social Impact</u>**

<u>Wars of Religion</u> The Reformation sparked conflicts such as the Thirty Years' War, leading to significant political and social upheavals.

<u>Religious Toleration</u> In some regions, the Reformation contributed to the development of principles of religious toleration and individual freedom.

3. **<u>Interconnections</u>** The Renaissance and Reformation were interconnected movements, with the revival of classical learning contributing to a critical examination of religious practices and beliefs.

Humanist scholars often played roles in both movements, advocating for intellectual inquiry, critical thinking, and a return to original sources in both religious and secular contexts.

The Renaissance and Reformation collectively transformed the intellectual, religious, and cultural landscape of Europe, laying the groundwork for the modern era. They challenged established norms, encouraged individual inquiry, and contributed to the emergence of diverse religious traditions.

Chapter 9

<u>Age of Exploration</u>

The Age of Exploration, also known as the Age of Discovery, was a period from the late 15th century to the early 17th century during which European powers embarked on maritime expeditions to explore and establish trade routes to new lands. This era was marked by significant advancements in navigation, technology, and cartography, leading to the discovery of previously unknown territories and the establishment of global connections. Here's a detailed exploration of the Age of Exploration,

1. **Background**

Trade Routes Prior to the Age of Exploration, European merchants sought direct access to the lucrative trade routes of Asia, bypassing intermediaries in the Middle East.

Technological Advancements Developments such as the compass, astrolabe, and caravel (a versatile sailing ship) improved navigation and made long-distance sea voyages more feasible.

2. **Portuguese Exploration**

Prince Henry the Navigator Prince Henry of Portugal played a key role in promoting maritime exploration. He established a navigation school and sponsored expeditions along the African coast.

Cape of Good Hope In 1488, Bartholomeu Dias successfully rounded the Cape of Good Hope, opening a sea route to the Indian Ocean.

3. **Christopher Columbus and the Americas**

Voyages of Columbus Christopher Columbus, sponsored by Spain, undertook four voyages between 1492 and 1504, reaching the islands of the Caribbean and the coasts of Central and South America.

Impact Columbus's voyages marked the beginning of European exploration and colonization in the Americas.

4. **Vasco da Gama and the Sea Route to India**

Voyage to India Vasco da Gama, in 1497-1499, successfully sailed around the Cape of Good Hope and reached the shores of Calicut in India, establishing a sea route to Asia.

Impact on Trade The direct sea route to India bypassed overland trade routes controlled by Middle Eastern merchants, enhancing European access to valuable goods.

5. **Spanish Conquistadors and Conquest of the Americas**

Conquistadors Spanish explorers, known as conquistadors, including Hernán Cortés and Francisco Pizarro, undertook expeditions to the Americas, leading to the conquest of the Aztec and Inca civilizations.

Search for Wealth Conquistadors sought gold, silver, and other valuable resources, contributing to the economic wealth of Spain.

6. **Treaty of Tordesillas (1494)**

Division of Territories To avoid conflicts between Spain and Portugal, the Treaty of Tordesillas divided the non-European world into Spanish and Portuguese spheres of influence along a meridian in the Atlantic Ocean.

Impact on Colonization This treaty influenced the territories each country explored and colonized in the Americas, Africa, and Asia.

7. **Exploration by Other European Powers**

Dutch and English Explorers Dutch and English explorers, such as Henry Hudson and John Cabot, sought Northwest and Northeast Passage routes to Asia, respectively.

Colonization in North America The English established colonies in North America, including Jamestown in 1607 and Plymouth in 1620.

8. **Trade and the Columbian Exchange**

Columbian Exchange The exchange of goods, animals, plants, and diseases between the Old World and the New World had profound ecological, economic, and cultural impacts.

Introduction of New Crops The transfer of crops like maize, potatoes, and tomatoes transformed agricultural practices on both continents.

9. **Impact on Indigenous Peoples**

Cultural Exchange Interactions between Europeans and indigenous peoples led to cultural exchanges, but also to conflicts and the spread of diseases, resulting in significant population declines.

Colonization and Cultural Transformation European colonization led to the establishment of new societies in the Americas, blending European, indigenous, and African cultures.

10. **Legacy**

Global Trade Networks The Age of Exploration laid the foundation for global trade networks, connecting Europe, the Americas, Africa, and Asia in a complex system of exchange.

Colonial Empires European nations established vast colonial empires, shaping the geopolitical landscape for centuries to come.

The Age of Exploration had far-reaching consequences, influencing trade, geopolitics, and cultural interactions on a global scale.

Chapter 10

<u>Enlightenment</u>

The Enlightenment, also known as the Age of Enlightenment, was an intellectual and cultural movement that emerged in Europe during the late 17th to 18th centuries. This period was characterized by a focus on reason, science, individualism, and skepticism of traditional authority. Enlightenment thinkers sought to apply the principles of reason and empiricism to understand and improve human society, government, and the natural world. Here's a detailed exploration of the Enlightenment.

1. **<u>Key Ideas and Themes</u>**

<u>Reason</u> Enlightenment thinkers emphasized the power of reason as a means of understanding the world and solving societal problems. They advocated for rational thought and scientific inquiry.

<u>Empiricism</u> The Enlightenment promoted the idea that knowledge should be derived from empirical evidence and observation, challenging reliance on religious dogma or tradition.

<u>Individualism</u> Enlightenment thinkers championed the value and rights of the individual. Concepts like personal liberty, autonomy, and individual rights became central to Enlightenment philosophy.

<u>Secularism</u> The Enlightenment sought to separate church and state, promoting secularism and advocating for the application of reason in politics and governance.

<u>Optimism and Progress</u> Enlightenment thinkers were generally optimistic about human progress. They believed that reason and science could lead to improvements in society, education, and government.

2. **<u>Scientific Revolution and Enlightenment</u>**

<u>Influence of Scientific Advances</u> The Scientific Revolution of the 16th and 17th centuries, with figures like Copernicus, Galileo, and Newton, laid the groundwork for Enlightenment thinking by promoting empirical observation and a scientific approach to understanding the natural world.

Encyclopedias Projects like the Encyclopédie, edited by Denis Diderot and Jean le Rond d'Alembert, sought to compile and disseminate knowledge across various disciplines, reflecting the Enlightenment emphasis on education and accessibility of information.

3. Enlightenment Thinkers

John Locke Locke's "Two Treatises of Government" (1690) argued for the natural rights of life, liberty, and property. His ideas influenced later thinkers and the development of constitutional governance.

Voltaire A prominent French philosopher and satirist, Voltaire championed free speech, religious tolerance, and criticism of oppressive institutions.

Montesquieu In "The Spirit of the Laws" (1748), Montesquieu advocated for the separation of powers within government to prevent tyranny and protect individual freedoms.

Jean-Jacques Rousseau Rousseau's "The Social Contract" (1762) discussed the idea of a social contract and the importance of popular sovereignty in governance.

4. Political Philosophy

Social Contract Enlightenment thinkers explored the concept of the social contract, where individuals willingly submit to a government in exchange for protection of their natural rights. Rousseau, Locke, and others contributed to this discourse.

Ideas on Government Enlightenment ideas influenced the development of democratic principles and constitutional government. The U.S. Constitution, with its checks and balances, reflected Enlightenment thinking.

5. Impact on Religion

Religious Toleration Enlightenment thinkers advocated for religious tolerance and freedom of thought. They challenged religious dogma and called for the separation of church and state.

Deism Some Enlightenment figures embraced deism, a belief in a distant, non-interventionist God who created the universe but did not actively govern it.

6. Education and Enlightenment

Emphasis on Education Enlightenment thinkers believed in the transformative power of education. They advocated for universal education to empower individuals and promote enlightened values.

Salons and Coffeehouses Intellectual discussions flourished in salons and coffeehouses, where thinkers, writers, and philosophers exchanged ideas, fostering a sense of intellectual community.

7. Critique of Absolute Monarchy

Limiting Absolute Power Enlightenment thinkers criticized absolute monarchy and the unchecked power of rulers. They proposed constitutional limits on governmental authority to protect individual rights.

8. Legacy of the Enlightenment

Influence on Revolutions Enlightenment ideas influenced political revolutions, including the American Revolution (1775–1783) and the French Revolution (1789–1799), shaping the development of democratic institutions.

Human Rights The Enlightenment laid the groundwork for the development of the concept of human rights, emphasizing the inherent dignity and equality of all individuals.

The Enlightenment was a transformative period that had a profound impact on the intellectual, cultural, and political development of Western societies. Its emphasis on reason, individual rights, and progress contributed to the shaping of modern democratic ideals and institutions.

Chapter 11

Industrial Revolution

The Industrial Revolution was a period of profound economic, technological, and social change that began in Britain in the late 18th century and spread to other parts of the world during the 19th and early 20th centuries. It marked a shift from agrarian and craft-based economies to industrialized, machine-driven production. The Industrial Revolution had far-reaching impacts on every aspect of society, including economic structures, living conditions, and labor relations. Here's a detailed exploration of the Industrial Revolution.

1. **Origins and Early Developments**

Textile Industry The Industrial Revolution began in the textile sector, with innovations such as the spinning jenny, water frame, and power loom. These inventions mechanized the production of textiles, significantly increasing efficiency.

Invention of the Steam Engine The development of the steam engine by James Watt in the 1760s marked a crucial advancement. It provided a new, efficient source of power for machinery and transformed various industries.

2. **Mechanization of Industry**

Factory System The factory system emerged, bringing together workers and machines under one roof. Factories replaced cottage industries, leading to increased production and centralization of manufacturing.

Division of Labor The division of labor became more specialized, with workers assigned specific tasks in the production process, enhancing efficiency but often resulting in monotonous and repetitive work.

3. **Technological Innovations**

Railways The expansion of railways revolutionized transportation, allowing for faster and more reliable movement of goods and people.

Telegraph The invention of the telegraph improved communication, enabling rapid transmission of information over long distances.

Steel Production The Bessemer process, developed in the mid-19th century, made mass steel production more economical, leading to the growth of industries like construction and transportation.

4. **Impact on Agriculture**

Mechanized Agriculture Agricultural practices were transformed with the introduction of machinery such as the mechanical reaper and seed drill, leading to increased productivity.

Urbanization As agricultural labor needs decreased due to mechanization, people migrated from rural areas to urban centers in search of employment in factories.

5. **Social and Economic Changes**

Population Growth Improved living conditions, nutrition, and healthcare contributed to a significant increase in population.

Urbanization Cities grew rapidly as people moved from rural areas to urban centers for work. However, urbanization also brought about challenges like overcrowded housing, poor sanitation, and social issues.

Rise of the Middle Class The Industrial Revolution led to the emergence of a middle class, including industrialists, professionals, and managers.

6. **Labor Conditions**

Factory Working Conditions Factory work was characterized by long hours, low wages, and often hazardous conditions. Workers, including women and children, faced challenging labor conditions.

Labor Movements Over time, labor movements and unions emerged to advocate for workers' rights and improved working conditions.

7. **Global Impact**

Spread of Industrialization The Industrial Revolution spread to other parts of Europe, North America, and eventually to Asia, transforming global economic structures.

Imperialism Industrialized nations sought resources and markets through imperialism, impacting the economic and political structures of colonized regions.

8. Economic Shifts

Capitalism The Industrial Revolution contributed to the development of capitalist economic systems, characterized by private ownership of the means of production and a market-driven economy.

Economic Growth Despite social and environmental challenges, the Industrial Revolution played a key role in fostering economic growth and technological innovation.

9. Environmental Impact

Pollution The rapid industrialization led to increased pollution, deforestation, and environmental degradation.

Resource Extraction The demand for raw materials led to extensive resource extraction, affecting ecosystems and landscapes.

10. Technological and Scientific Progress

Advancements in Science The Industrial Revolution was closely linked to advancements in science and technology, with figures like James Watt, Michael Faraday, and Thomas Edison making significant contributions.

Innovation Culture The era marked a shift toward an innovation culture, encouraging experimentation and the application of scientific principles to practical problems.

The Industrial Revolution was a transformative period that reshaped economies, societies, and daily life. While it brought about significant advancements and economic growth, it also raised social, environmental, and ethical concerns. Its impact continues to influence the modern world in various ways.

Chapter 12

<u>**American Revolution**</u>

The American Revolution was a pivotal event that took place between 1775 and 1783, leading to the thirteen American colonies gaining independence from British rule and forming the United States of America. The revolution was fueled by a combination of political, economic, social, and ideological factors, and it had far-reaching consequences for the United States and the broader world. Here's a detailed exploration of the American Revolution.

1. <u>**Background and Causes**</u>

<u>**Taxation Without Representation**</u> Tensions rose over British taxation policies, such as the Stamp Act (1765) and the Townshend Acts (1767), which the colonists deemed unfair as they lacked representation in the British Parliament.

<u>**Boston Massacre (1770)**</u> The killing of colonists by British soldiers heightened resentment and fueled anti-British sentiments.

<u>**Boston Tea Party (1773)**</u> Colonists protested the Tea Act by throwing British tea into Boston Harbor, leading to increased British repression and further colonial resistance.

2. <u>**Outbreak of Hostilities**</u>

<u>**Lexington and Concord (1775)**</u> The first military engagements of the revolution occurred at Lexington and Concord, Massachusetts, when British troops clashed with colonial militias. This marked the beginning of armed conflict.

3. <u>**Continental Congress and Declaration of Independence**</u>

<u>**Second Continental Congress (1775)**</u> The representatives from the colonies convened to address grievances and organize a defense against British forces.

Declaration of Independence (1776) Thomas Jefferson drafted the Declaration of Independence, asserting the colonies' right to self-government and listing grievances against King George III. It was adopted on July 4, 1776.

4. **Military Campaigns**

Siege of Boston The Continental Army, led by George Washington, forced the British to evacuate Boston in 1776.

Battle of Saratoga (1777) A decisive American victory over the British boosted American morale and led to France formally entering the war as an ally to the American cause.

Winter at Valley Forge (1777–1778) The Continental Army faced harsh conditions, but training and discipline improved under Baron von Steuben.

Siege of Yorktown (1781) Combined American and French forces laid siege to Yorktown, leading to the surrender of British General Cornwallis and effectively ending major military operations.

5. **Treaty of Paris (1783)**

Recognition of Independence The Treaty of Paris officially ended the war and recognized the independence of the United States.

Territorial Changes The treaty established the Mississippi River as the western boundary, with the United States gaining territory east of the river.

6. **Impact on Global Politics**

Inspiration for Revolutions The success of the American Revolution inspired movements for independence and democracy in other parts of the world, including Latin America and Europe.

7. **Formation of the United States**

Articles of Confederation (1781) The first constitution of the United States established a weak central government, and it was later replaced by the U.S. Constitution in 1787.

Bill of Rights (1791) The first ten amendments to the U.S. Constitution, known as the Bill of Rights, were added to protect individual liberties.

8. Political and Social Changes

Republicanism The revolution fostered a republican ideology emphasizing representative government and the importance of civic virtue.

Abolition of Monarchy The United States rejected monarchy in favor of a democratic republic.

9. Challenges and Debates

Debates over Slavery Despite principles of liberty, the institution of slavery persisted, leading to ongoing debates and conflicts that would culminate in the Civil War.

Women's Rights While the revolution did not immediately lead to significant gains in women's rights, it sparked discussions about equality and laid groundwork for future movements.

10. Legacy

Founding Documents The Declaration of Independence and the U.S. Constitution became foundational documents, shaping the principles of American democracy.

National Identity The American Revolution played a crucial role in shaping the national identity of the United States, emphasizing values such as freedom, democracy, and individual rights.

The American Revolution was a transformative period that laid the groundwork for the establishment of the United States as a sovereign nation. It inspired democratic movements worldwide and contributed to the evolution of political and social ideologies in the centuries that followed.

Chapter 13

French Revolution

The French Revolution was a period of radical social and political upheaval in France that lasted from 1789 to 1799. It marked the end of absolute monarchy and the rise of radical political ideologies, including republicanism and nationalism. The revolution had far-reaching consequences, not only for France but also for the rest of Europe. Here's a detailed exploration of the French Revolution.

1. **Background and Causes**

Financial Crisis France faced severe financial difficulties due to wars, extravagant spending by the monarchy, and an inefficient tax system.

Social Inequality A rigid social structure characterized by privileges for the nobility and clergy, while the common people faced heavy taxation and economic hardship.

Enlightenment Ideas Enlightenment philosophies advocating for reason, equality, and individual rights influenced revolutionary thought.

2. **Estates-General and National Assembly**

Estates-General (1789) King Louis XVI convened the Estates-General to address the financial crisis. Disputes over voting led to the formation of the National Assembly by representatives of the Third Estate (common people).

Tennis Court Oath (1789) The National Assembly, locked out of its usual meeting place, pledged to continue meeting until a new constitution was established.

3. **Storming of the Bastille (July 14, 1789)**

Symbolic Event The storming of the Bastille, a royal prison, became a symbol of the people's defiance against royal authority and is considered the start of the revolution.

Formation of the Paris Commune The revolutionary spirit spread to Paris, leading to the formation of the Paris Commune.

4. <u>Abolition of Feudalism and Declaration of Rights of Man and Citizen</u>

<u>**National Assembly Reforms**</u> The National Assembly abolished feudal privileges and drafted the Declaration of Rights of Man and Citizen, asserting individual rights, equality, and popular sovereignty.

<u>**Constitution of 1791**</u> A new constitution established a constitutional monarchy, limiting the king's powers.

5. <u>Radical Phase and Reign of Terror</u>

<u>**Radicalization**</u> The revolution entered a more radical phase with the rise of political clubs like the Jacobins and the Cordeliers.

<u>**Execution of Louis XVI (1793):**</u> King Louis XVI was executed, symbolizing the rejection of monarchy and the establishment of the First French Republic.

<u>**Committee of Public Safety**</u> Maximilien Robespierre and the Committee of Public Safety emerged, leading to the Reign of Terror, marked by mass executions of perceived enemies of the revolution.

<u>**Execution of Robespierre (1794)**</u> Robespierre's radicalism led to his downfall, and he was executed, marking the end of the Reign of Terror.

6. <u>Rise of Napoleon Bonaparte</u>

<u>**Directory and Instability**</u> The revolution led to political instability, and the Directory, the government that followed, faced challenges.

<u>**Coup d'État of 18 Brumaire (1799)**</u> Napoleon Bonaparte staged a coup, leading to the establishment of the Consulate and eventually making himself First Consul.

7. <u>Napoleonic Era</u>

Napoleonic Code Napoleon implemented legal reforms, including the Napoleonic Code, which had a lasting impact on European legal systems.

Expansion and Wars Napoleon expanded French territory through military conquests across Europe.

Downfall (1814) Napoleon's military defeats, including the Battle of Leipzig, led to his abdication and exile to the island of Elba.

8. **Legacy**

Impact on Europe The French Revolution inspired nationalist movements and challenged established monarchies across Europe.

Spread of Revolutionary Ideals Ideas of liberty, equality, and fraternity spread globally, influencing subsequent revolutionary movements.

9. **Social and Cultural Changes**

Secularization The revolution led to the secularization of French society, with the Church losing its privileged status.

Cultural Transformation The revolution influenced art, literature, and cultural expression, reflecting themes of liberty and nationalism.

10. **Challenges and Unfinished Business**

Political Turmoil France faced ongoing political turbulence, with changes in government and shifting power dynamics.

Napoleonic Wars The Napoleonic Wars, spanning from 1803 to 1815, had profound consequences for Europe, reshaping borders and political structures.

The French Revolution, while marked by ideals of liberty and equality, also witnessed intense internal conflicts, violence, and shifts in political power. Its legacy continues to be debated, with historians recognizing its role in shaping modern political ideologies and institutions.

Chapter 14

<u>Napoleonic Era</u>

The Napoleonic Era refers to the period of French and European history that unfolded during the rule of Napoleon Bonaparte, a military and political leader who rose to prominence during the French Revolution. Napoleon's influence extended from the late 18th century to the early 19th century, shaping the political, social, and military landscape of Europe. Here's a detailed exploration of the Napoleonic Era.

1. **<u>Rise to Power</u>**

<u>Military Success</u> Napoleon rose through the ranks of the French military during the French Revolution, demonstrating strategic brilliance in campaigns such as the Italian and Egyptian campaigns.

<u>Coup d'État of 18 Brumaire (1799)</u> Faced with political instability in France, Napoleon orchestrated a coup d'État on November 9, 1799 (18 Brumaire in the French Republican calendar), leading to the establishment of the Consulate. This marked the end of the French Revolution and the beginning of Napoleon's political ascendancy.

2. **<u>Consolidation of Power</u>**

<u>Constitutional Changes</u> Napoleon implemented several constitutional changes, consolidating power in the hands of the executive. In 1804, he established the French Consulate and, in 1804, became Emperor Napoleon I.

<u>Napoleonic Code</u> Napoleon enacted the Napoleonic Code (Code Napoléon), a comprehensive legal code that influenced legal systems across Europe. It emphasized principles of equality, individual rights, and legal certainty.

3. **<u>Military Campaigns and Expansion</u>**

<u>Wars of the Third Coalition (1805)</u> Napoleon defeated the Austro-Russian forces at the Battle of Austerlitz, establishing French dominance.

Peninsular War (1808–1814) Conflict erupted in the Iberian Peninsula, as Napoleon sought to assert control, leading to a protracted war against Spanish and Portuguese forces.

Invasion of Russia (1812) Napoleon's ill-fated invasion of Russia resulted in catastrophic losses for the French army due to harsh winter conditions and Russian scorched-earth tactics.

War of the Sixth Coalition (1812–1814) The European powers, including Russia, Prussia, Austria, and the United Kingdom, formed coalitions against France, leading to Napoleon's decline.

4. Downfall and Exile

Defeat at Leipzig (1813) The Battle of Leipzig, also known as the Battle of Nations, marked a significant defeat for Napoleon, forcing his retreat from German territories.

Exile to Elba (1814) Following his abdication in 1814, Napoleon was exiled to the island of Elba in the Mediterranean. The Bourbon monarchy was restored in France under Louis XVIII.

5. Hundred Days

Return from Exile (1815) Napoleon escaped from Elba in 1815 and returned to France for a brief period known as the Hundred Days.

Defeat at Waterloo (1815) Napoleon faced a coalition army led by the Duke of Wellington and was decisively defeated at the Battle of Waterloo in Belgium.

6. Second Abdication and Exile to St. Helena

Second Abdication (1815) After the defeat at Waterloo, Napoleon abdicated for the second time on June 22, 1815.

Exile to St. Helena The British government exiled Napoleon to the remote island of St. Helena in the South Atlantic, where he remained until his death in 1821.

7. Legacy

Impact on Europe The Napoleonic Wars reshaped the political map of Europe, leading to territorial adjustments, the redrawing of borders, and the establishment of new political entities.

Spread of Nationalism Napoleon's campaigns contributed to the spread of nationalism, as the notion of a shared identity and loyalty to a nation gained momentum.

Legal Reforms The Napoleonic Code continued to influence legal systems, promoting principles of equality and individual rights.

8. **Congress of Vienna (1814–1815)**

Restoration of Monarchies European powers convened at the Congress of Vienna to restore monarchies and redraw territorial boundaries, aiming to maintain stability after the Napoleonic upheavals.

Balance of Power The Congress sought to establish a balance of power in Europe to prevent future conflicts.

9. **Return of the Bourbon Monarchy**

Restoration of Louis XVIII The Bourbon monarchy was restored in France with the return of Louis XVIII to the throne after Napoleon's defeat.

The Napoleonic Era left an enduring impact on European history, influencing legal systems, political ideologies, and the concept of nationalism. Napoleon's military prowess, administrative reforms, and the subsequent efforts to restore stability in Europe after his downfall shaped the trajectory of the continent in the 19th century.

Chapter 15

<u>19th Century Nationalism</u>

The 19th-century was a period marked by the rise of nationalism, a political and social movement characterized by the identification and promotion of a shared national identity, culture, and political sovereignty. Nationalism played a significant role in shaping the political landscape of Europe and other parts of the world during this era. Here's a detailed exploration of 19th-century nationalism.

1. Historical Context

Post-Napoleonic Europe The Napoleonic Wars and the Congress of Vienna (1814–1815) reshaped European boundaries and political structures, fostering a climate of political reorganization and realignment.

Impact of Enlightenment and Romanticism Ideas of the Enlightenment, emphasizing individual rights and democratic principles, combined with the emotional and cultural emphasis of Romanticism, contributed to the rise of nationalist sentiments.

2. Characteristics of 19th-Century Nationalism

Cultural Identity Nationalism emphasized a shared cultural identity, including language, history, traditions, and symbols.

Political Sovereignty Nationalists sought political sovereignty and self-determination for their distinct national communities.

Anti-Imperial Sentiment Nationalist movements often emerged in opposition to imperial rule and foreign domination.

3. Unification Movements

Italy Giuseppe Mazzini, Giuseppe Garibaldi, and Count Camillo Cavour played key roles in the Italian unification (Risorgimento) process, leading to the creation of a unified Kingdom of Italy in 1861.

Germany The German states, led by figures like Otto von Bismarck, underwent a process of unification known as the German Empire, established in 1871.

4. <u>Independence Movements</u>

<u>Greece</u> The Greek War of Independence (1821–1829) led to the establishment of the modern Greek state, supported by philhellenes and inspired by ancient Greek ideals.

<u>Latin American Nations</u> Various Latin American nations, including Mexico, Brazil, and the countries in the Andean region, gained independence from Spanish and Portuguese colonial rule during the early 19th century.

5. <u>Nationalism in Eastern Europe</u>

<u>Poland</u> Nationalism played a role in Polish uprisings against Russian, Prussian, and Austrian rule, although full Polish independence was not achieved until after World War I.

<u>Czech and Slovak Nationalism</u> Nationalist sentiments among Czechs and Slovaks contributed to the emergence of Czechoslovakia as an independent state after World War I.

6. <u>Nationalism in the Ottoman Empire</u>

<u>Balkan Nationalism</u> Nationalist movements in the Balkans sought independence from Ottoman rule, leading to a series of conflicts and the eventual emergence of independent states.

7. <u>Challenges and Conflicts</u>

<u>Competing Nationalisms</u> The rise of nationalism often led to conflicts between different national groups, as seen in the Austro-Hungarian Empire, Ottoman Empire, and other multi-ethnic states.

<u>Irredentism</u> Nationalist movements sought to unite regions with shared cultural and ethnic ties, contributing to tensions and conflicts.

8. <u>Impact on European Politics</u>

<u>Balance of Power</u> Nationalism influenced the balance of power in Europe, as newly unified states emerged and sought to assert their interests.

Decline of Empires The Ottoman, Austro-Hungarian, and Russian Empires faced challenges from nationalist movements that sought independence or autonomy for various ethnic groups.

9. **Cultural Expression** Nationalist sentiments found expression in literature, music, and the arts. Romantic composers, such as Wagner, often drew inspiration from national themes.

10. **Legacy and Challenges**

Legacy of Nationalism: The 19th-century nationalist movements left a lasting impact on the political map of Europe and beyond, influencing the formation of nation-states.

Challenges and Conflicts While nationalism contributed to the formation of independent states, it also sparked conflicts, territorial disputes, and challenges related to ethnic and cultural diversity.

The 19th-century nationalist movements were a complex and transformative force that reshaped political boundaries, challenged imperial rule, and contributed to the formation of nation-states. However, the legacy of nationalism also included challenges related to competing national interests.

Chapter 16

Colonialism

Colonialism refers to the establishment, maintenance, and expansion of colonies in one territory by people from another territory, usually for economic, political, and cultural purposes. It is a historical phenomenon that has shaped the development of societies and nations, with significant implications for both the colonizers and the colonized. Here's a detailed exploration of colonialism.

1. **Motivations for Colonialism**

Economic Exploitation Many colonial powers sought to exploit the resources of the colonized territories, including valuable minerals, agricultural products, and labor.

Trade Routes Control of strategic trade routes and access to new markets were key motivations for establishing colonies.

Political Power Colonial expansion often served as a means of enhancing a nation's political power and influence on the global stage.

Missionary and Civilizing Efforts Some colonial powers claimed a moral duty to spread their culture, religion, and civilization to what they considered less developed societies.

2. **Types of Colonialism**

Settler Colonialism In settler colonies, the colonizers established permanent communities, displacing or subjugating the indigenous populations. Eg. - North America, Australia, and parts of Africa.

Exploitation Colonies In exploitation colonies, the primary goal was the extraction of resources and wealth, often without significant efforts to establish permanent settlements. Examples include many parts of Africa and Asia during the era of European imperialism.

3. **European Colonialism**

Age of Exploration The Age of Exploration in the 15th to 17th centuries marked the beginning of European colonial expansion, with Portugal, England, Spain, the Netherlands, and France leading the way.

Scramble for Africa In the late 19th and early 20th centuries, European powers engaged in the "Scramble for Africa," resulting in the colonization of almost the entire continent.

4. **Impact on Indigenous Peoples**

Cultural Disruption Colonialism often led to the disruption and erasure of indigenous cultures, languages, and traditions.

Land Displacement Indigenous populations frequently faced displacement from their ancestral lands, sometimes through forceful means.

Economic Exploitation The colonized territories were often economically exploited for the benefit of the colonizers, leading to significant disparities in wealth and development.

5. **Colonial Administration**

Direct Rule Some colonial powers implemented direct rule, where they governed the colonies through appointed officials from the colonizing country.

Indirect Rule Other colonial powers adopted indirect rule, allowing local leaders to govern under the supervision of colonial authorities.

6. **Resistance and Independence Movements**

Colonial Resistance Indigenous populations frequently resisted colonial rule through various means, including armed resistance, cultural preservation, and diplomatic efforts.

Independence Movements The mid 20th century witnessed a wave of decolonization, as many colonies gained independence through diplomatic negotiations, armed struggles, or combination of both.

7. **Legacy of Colonialism**

Borders and Boundaries The artificial borders drawn by colonial powers often did not align with the cultural or ethnic divisions of the indigenous populations, leading to ongoing conflicts in some regions.

Economic Inequalities Colonial legacies contributed to economic disparities between former colonies and their colonizers, impacting issues such as poverty and development.

Cultural Hybridity In some cases, colonialism led to cultural hybridity, where indigenous cultures merged with aspects of the colonizers' cultures, creating unique identities.

8. Post-Colonial Challenges

Nation-Building Many post-colonial nations faced the challenge of building stable and inclusive political structures that could accommodate diverse ethnic, religious, and linguistic groups.

Economic Development Post-colonial nations often had to contend with economic challenges, including debt, resource exploitation, and unequal global trade relationships.

Colonialism, while shaping the course of history and contributing to global interconnectedness, is also associated with significant injustices, exploitation, and legacies that continue to influence the modern world. The study of colonialism involves examining the complexities and consequences of interactions between colonizers and colonized societies.

Chapter 17

<u>World War I</u>

World War I, also known as the Great War, was a global conflict that lasted from July 28, 1914, to November 11, 1918. It involved many of the world's great powers and spanned multiple continents, making it one of the largest and deadliest conflicts in history up to that point. Here's a detailed exploration of World War I.

1. **Causes of World War I**

Assassination of Archduke Franz Ferdinand The assassination of Archduke Franz Ferdinand of Austria-Hungary in Sarajevo on June 28, 1914, was the immediate trigger for the war.

Alliance Systems The complex system of military alliances in Europe, including the Triple Entente (France, Russia, and the United Kingdom) and the Triple Alliance (Germany, Austria-Hungary, and Italy), created a web of obligations that drew multiple nations into the conflict.

Imperialism Competition for colonies and global influence among European powers heightened tensions.

Nationalism Intense nationalism fueled a desire for territorial expansion and contributed to the willingness of nations to go to war.

Militarism The buildup of military forces and an arms race added to the overall atmosphere of militarism in Europe.

2. **Key Participants**

Allied Powers (Entente) France, Russia, the United Kingdom, and later joined by Italy, the United States, and others.

Central Powers Germany, Austria-Hungary, the Ottoman Empire, and Bulgaria.

3. **Major Battles and Campaigns**

Western Front Trench warfare characterized the Western Front, with major battles including the Battle of the Marne, Battle of Verdun, and the Battle of the Somme.

Eastern Front Eastern Europe witnessed large-scale battles, with notable conflicts at Tannenberg and the Brusilov Offensive.

Gallipoli Campaign Allied forces, mainly from Australia and New Zealand, attempted to capture the Gallipoli Peninsula to secure a sea route to Russia but faced heavy losses.

Italian Front Battles between Italy and Austria-Hungary, including the Battle of Caporetto.

4. Warfare and Technology

Trench Warfare Stalemate on the Western Front led to the development of extensive trench systems, resulting in a brutal and protracted form of warfare.

New Weapons The war saw the introduction of new weapons, including machine guns, tanks, poison gas, and aircraft, transforming the nature of combat.

5. U.S. Entry into the War

Lusitania and Unrestricted Submarine Warfare The sinking of the British ocean liner Lusitania by a German submarine in 1915, and the resumption of unrestricted submarine warfare by Germany, contributed to the United States entering the war in 1917.

Zimmermann Telegram The interception of a German diplomatic communication proposing a military alliance with Mexico against the U.S. further swayed public opinion in the United States.

6. Russian Revolution (1917)

Bolshevik Takeover The Russian Revolution led to the Bolsheviks seizing power in October 1917, resulting in Russia's withdrawal from the war after signing the Treaty of Brest-Litovsk with the Central Powers in 1918.

7. Armistice and Treaty of Versailles

Armistice On November 11, 1918, an armistice was signed, bringing an end to the fighting on the Western Front.

Treaty of Versailles (1919) The peace treaty signed at the Palace of Versailles imposed harsh terms on Germany, including territorial losses, disarmament, and reparations, contributing to long-term geopolitical tensions.

8. **Consequences and Legacy**

Casualties The war resulted in millions of casualties, both military and civilian, with widespread physical and psychological trauma.

Political Changes The war led to the collapse of empires (Austro-Hungarian, Ottoman, German, and Russian) and the redrawing of national boundaries.

League of Nations The League of Nations, established in the aftermath of the war, aimed to prevent future conflicts but faced challenges and ultimately proved ineffective.

Precursor to World War II The unresolved issues and grievances from World War I set the stage for World War II, as the harsh terms of the Treaty of Versailles and geopolitical tensions contributed to later conflicts.

World War I had profound and far-reaching effects on the 20th century, shaping the geopolitical landscape, influencing political ideologies, and laying the groundwork for subsequent global events.

Chapter 18

<u>Russian Revolution</u>

The Russian Revolution refers to the series of events that took place in Russia in 1917, leading to the overthrow of the Romanov dynasty and the establishment of a socialist government under the Bolshevik Party. The revolution had a profound impact on Russia and the course of 20th-century history. Here's a detailed exploration of the Russian Revolution.

1. **<u>Background</u>**

<u>Tsarist Rule</u> Russia was ruled by an autocratic monarchy under the Romanov dynasty. Tsar Nicholas II was the last ruler, and his reign was marked by political repression, economic hardship, and military failures, especially during World War I.

<u>Social and Economic Inequality</u> The majority of the population faced poverty, while the aristocracy and the bourgeoisie held significant wealth and privileges.

<u>World War I</u> Russia's involvement in World War I strained resources and contributed to widespread discontent, as the war effort led to economic hardship and high casualties.

2. **<u>February Revolution (1917)</u>**

<u>Bread Riots</u> Widespread food shortages and discontent among urban workers and soldiers culminated in protests and strikes in Petrograd (St. Petersburg) in February 1917.

<u>Abdication of the Tsar</u> Faced with mounting pressure, Tsar Nicholas II abdicated on March 2, 1917, bringing an end to the Romanov dynasty.

3. **<u>Provisional Government</u>**

Formation The Provisional Government, composed mainly of liberals and moderate socialists, was established after the abdication of the tsar.

Challenges The Provisional Government faced challenges such as continuing the war, land reform, and addressing economic issues.

4. April Theses and Bolshevik Rise

Return of Lenin Vladimir Lenin, leader of the Bolshevik Party, returned to Russia from exile in April 1917.

April Theses Lenin presented the April Theses, outlining the Bolshevik agenda, which included calls for "Peace, Land, and Bread," as well as the transfer of power to the soviets (councils of workers and soldiers).

5. July Days (1917)

Protests and Suppression Mass protests erupted in Petrograd in July 1917, with workers and soldiers demanding an end to the war and land redistribution. The Provisional Government suppressed the uprising, and Lenin went into hiding.

6. October Revolution (1917)

Bolshevik Seizure of Power In October 1917 (Julian calendar; November in the Gregorian calendar), the Bolsheviks, led by Lenin and Leon Trotsky, seized key locations in Petrograd, including the Winter Palace.

Storming of the Winter Palace The Bolsheviks stormed the Winter Palace, the seat of the Provisional Government, leading to its downfall.

Establishment of Soviet Power The Second All-Russian Congress of Soviets ratified the transfer of power to the Bolsheviks, marking the establishment of Soviet power.

7. Bolshevik Consolidation of Power

Treaty of Brest-Litovsk (1918) The Bolshevik government signed a peace treaty with the Central Powers, ending Russia's involvement in World War I but ceding significant territory to Germany and its allies.

Civil War (1918–1922) The Bolsheviks faced opposition from anti-Bolshevik forces, known as the White Army, leading to a protracted and devastating civil war.

8. **Creation of the Russian Soviet Federative Socialist Republic (RSFSR)**

Formation The RSFSR was proclaimed in 1917 as the first socialist state in the world.

Constitution of 1918 The Bolsheviks adopted a new constitution, reflecting socialist principles and establishing a government based on soviets.

9. **Death of the Romanovs (Royal Family)** In July 1918, the former tsar, Nicholas II, and his family were executed by Bolshevik authorities in Yekaterinburg.

10. **Legacy**

Formation of the Soviet Union The Russian Revolution laid the groundwork for the creation of the Soviet Union in 1922, comprising multiple socialist republics.

Communist Ideology The Bolsheviks, under Lenin's leadership, established a communist state, promoting socialist principles and advocating for the eventual establishment of a classless society.

The Russian Revolution marked a turning point in Russian history, leading to the establishment of the world's first socialist state. It had far-reaching consequences, influencing the course of the 20th century and shaping the geopolitics of the Cold War era.

Chapter 19

<u>Interwar Period</u>

The Interwar Period, often referred to as the interbellum or the interwar years, spans the time between the end of World War I in 1918 and the beginning of World War II in 1939. It was a complex and transformative period characterized by political, economic, social, and cultural developments as nations sought to rebuild and reshape the world order after the devastation of the First World War. Here's a detailed exploration of the Interwar Period.

1. **<u>Treaty of Versailles and Post-War Settlements</u>**

<u>Treaty of Versailles (1919)</u> The peace treaty signed at the end of World War I imposed harsh terms on Germany, leading to territorial losses, disarmament, and reparations.

<u>League of Nations</u> The League of Nations was established with the goal of preventing future conflicts, although its effectiveness was limited.

2. **<u>Economic Challenges</u>**

<u>Post-War Economic Turmoil</u> The war left many nations with significant economic challenges, including war debt, inflation, and unemployment.

<u>Great Depression (1929)</u> The global economy suffered a severe downturn in the late 1920s and early 1930s, leading to widespread unemployment and economic hardship.

3. **<u>Political Changes</u>**

<u>Weimar Republic</u> Germany transitioned to the democratic Weimar Republic, facing political instability and economic difficulties.

<u>Russian Revolution and Soviet Union</u> The Russian Revolution in 1917 led to the establishment of the Soviet Union under Bolshevik rule.

4. **<u>Rise of Totalitarianism</u>**

<u>Fascism in Italy</u> Benito Mussolini's fascist movement came to power in Italy in 1922, emphasizing authoritarian rule and nationalism.

Nazism in Germany Adolf Hitler's National Socialist German Workers' Party (Nazi Party) rose to power in Germany in 1933, promoting an extreme form of nationalism and anti-Semitism.

5. **Spanish Civil War (1936–1939)**

Political Struggle The conflict in Spain between Republicans (left-wing) and Nationalists (right-wing) became a precursor to larger ideological struggles in Europe.

Foreign Involvement The Spanish Civil War saw international involvement, with fascist and communist powers supporting opposing sides.

6. **Expansionism and Imperialism**

Japanese Expansion Japan expanded its empire in East Asia, invading Manchuria in 1931 and pursuing further aggression in China.

Italian Invasion of Ethiopia (1935) Italy, under Mussolini, invaded Ethiopia, violating the League of Nations.

German Expansion Hitler's aggressive foreign policy sought to overturn the Treaty of Versailles, leading to the reoccupation of the Rhineland in 1936 and the annexation of Austria (Anschluss) in 1938.

7. **Munich Agreement (1938)** Western powers, particularly Britain and France, followed a policy of appeasement in response to Hitler's territorial demands, culminating in the Munich Agreement, which allowed Germany to annex the Sudetenland.

8. **Interwar Literature and Art** The period witnessed significant cultural and artistic movements, including the Harlem Renaissance, Dadaism, Surrealism, and the Lost Generation in literature.

9. **Rearmament and Military Preparations**

Rearmament In defiance of the Treaty of Versailles, Germany engaged in a massive rearmament program under Hitler.

Military Buildup Other major powers also undertook military preparations in anticipation of future conflicts.

10. **Path to World War II**

<u>Invasion of Poland (1939)</u> The Interwar Period came to an end with the German invasion of Poland on September 1, 1939, marking the beginning of World War II.

<u>Soviet Invasion of Poland</u> Following a secret agreement with Nazi Germany, the Soviet Union invaded Poland from the east on September 17, 1939.

The Interwar Period was a time of profound political, economic, and cultural change, with the emergence of new ideologies, the rise of totalitarian regimes, and the reconfiguration of global power dynamics. The failures of the League of Nations, economic hardships, and the unresolved issues from World War I set the stage for the even more devastating conflict that would follow in the form of World War II.

Chapter 20

<u>World War II</u>

World War II (1939-1945) was a global conflict that involved most of the world's nations, including all of the great powers, organized into two opposing military alliances: the Allies, led primarily by the United States, the Soviet Union, the United Kingdom, and China; and the Axis, led by Nazi Germany, Italy, and Japan. It was the deadliest and most widespread war in history, resulting in significant geopolitical changes and shaping the post-war world. Here's a detailed exploration of World War II.

1. **<u>Causes of World War II</u>**

<u>Treaty of Versailles</u> The harsh terms imposed on Germany by the Treaty of Versailles after World War I contributed to economic hardship and resentment, providing a fertile ground for the rise of Adolf Hitler and the Nazi Party.

<u>Expansionism and Aggression</u> Aggressive territorial expansion by Nazi Germany in Europe, Italian expansion in Africa, and Japanese expansion in Asia created tensions and provoked conflicts.

<u>Appeasement</u> The policy of appeasement by Western powers in the face of aggressive actions, particularly the Munich Agreement in 1938, failed to prevent the outbreak of war.

2. **<u>Key Participants</u>**

<u>Axis Powers</u> Germany, Italy, Japan, and later Hungary, Romania, and Bulgaria.

<u>Allied Powers</u> The United States, the Soviet Union, the United Kingdom, China, and numerous other nations, including Canada, Australia, France, and others.

3. **<u>Major Theaters of War</u>**

<u>European Theater</u> Mainly characterized by the war in Western Europe, the Battle of Britain, the Eastern Front between Germany and the Soviet Union, and the D-Day invasion.

Pacific Theater Focused on the conflict between Japan and the Allies in the Pacific, including battles such as Midway, Guadalcanal, and Iwo Jima.

4. **Key Events and Battles**

Invasion of Poland (1939) Germany's invasion of Poland marked the beginning of World War II.

Battle of Britain (1940) The German Luftwaffe's air campaign against Britain, which was successfully repelled.

Operation Barbarossa (1941) Germany's invasion of the Soviet Union, leading to a brutal conflict on the Eastern Front.

Pearl Harbor (1941) Japan's surprise attack on the U.S. naval base in Hawaii, bringing the United States into the war.

D-Day (1944) The Allied invasion of Normandy, a significant turning point in the war in Western Europe.

Battle of Stalingrad (1942-1943) A pivotal and brutal battle on the Eastern Front, resulting in a Soviet victory.

Pacific Island-Hopping Campaign U.S. strategy of capturing strategically important islands in the Pacific, such as Guadalcanal and Iwo Jima.

5. **Holocaust and Genocide**

Nazi Persecution The systematic genocide carried out by the Nazis, known as the Holocaust, resulted in the mass murder of six million Jews and millions of others, including Romani people and Soviet POWs.

War Crimes War crimes and atrocities were committed by various Axis and Allied powers during the conflict.

6. **Home Fronts and Total War**

Civilian Mobilization The war effort required extensive civilian mobilization, with women entering the workforce and countries implementing rationing and other measures.

Bombing Campaigns Major cities were subjected to strategic bombing campaigns, causing widespread destruction and civilian casualties.

Internment The internment of Japanese Americans in the United States and the forced labor of civilians in occupied territories.

7. **Turning Points**

Midway (1942) The Battle of Midway in the Pacific marked a turning point, halting Japanese expansion.

Stalingrad (1943) The Soviet victory at the Battle of Stalingrad marked a turning point on the Eastern Front.

D-Day (1944) The successful Allied invasion of Normandy shifted the momentum in Western Europe.

8. **End of the War**

Battle of Berlin (1945) The Soviet Red Army's advance into Berlin led to the fall of Nazi Germany.

Atomic Bombs (1945) The United States dropped atomic bombs on the Japanese cities of Hiroshima and Nagasaki, leading to Japan's surrender.

9. **Consequences and Aftermath**

Formation of the United Nations The United Nations was established in 1945 to promote international cooperation and prevent future conflicts.

Division of Germany Germany was divided into East and West, with the Cold War emerging between the Soviet Union and the Western Allies.

War Crimes Trials The Nuremberg and Tokyo Trials held accountable individuals for war crimes and crimes against humanity.

Global Reordering The geopolitical landscape was dramatically reshaped, leading to the emergence of the United States and the Soviet Union as superpowers.

World War II resulted in unprecedented destruction and loss of life, leaving a lasting impact on the 20th century. It set the stage for the Cold War, the establishment of new nation-states, and significant changes in global power dynamics. The war's lessons continue to shape international relations and efforts to prevent conflict and promote peace.

Chapter 21

Cold War

The Cold War was a geopolitical and ideological confrontation between the United States and its Western allies, on one side, and the Soviet Union and its Eastern Bloc allies, on the other, that lasted roughly from the end of World War II in 1945 to the collapse of the Soviet Union in 1991. While direct military conflict between the two superpowers was avoided, the Cold War involved intense political, economic, ideological, and military rivalry. Here's a detailed exploration of the Cold War.

1. **Origins**

End of World War II The wartime alliance between the U.S., the Soviet Union, and other Allies against Nazi Germany and Japan began to unravel as ideological and geopolitical differences emerged.

Yalta and Potsdam Conferences The post-war conferences highlighted differences in the approaches of the Allies, particularly regarding the future of Eastern Europe.

2. **Ideological Conflict**

Capitalism vs. Communism The Cold War was characterized by the ideological clash between capitalism, led by the United States, and communism, led by the Soviet Union.

Iron Curtain Winston Churchill's famous "Iron Curtain" speech in 1946 described the division of Europe into Soviet-controlled Eastern Europe and the democratic West.

3. **Military Alliances**

NATO (North Atlantic Treaty Organization) Formed in 1949, NATO was a military alliance of Western countries, including the U.S. and European nations, aimed at countering the perceived threat from the Soviet Union.

Warsaw Pact Established in 1955, the Warsaw Pact was a military alliance of Soviet-controlled Eastern European countries in response to NATO.

4. <u>Arms Race</u>

<u>**Nuclear Weapons**</u> Both the U.S. and the Soviet Union developed and stockpiled nuclear weapons, leading to a nuclear arms race and the concept of mutually assured destruction (MAD).

<u>**Space Race**</u> The competition extended into space exploration, with the Soviet Union launching the first artificial satellite, Sputnik, in 1957, and the U.S. landing the first humans on the moon in 1969.

5. <u>Proxy Wars</u>

<u>**Korean War (1950-1953)**</u> The conflict between North Korea (supported by China and the Soviet Union) and South Korea (backed by the U.S. and its allies) exemplified the use of proxy wars during the Cold War.

<u>**Vietnam War (1955-1975)**</u> The Vietnam War was a protracted conflict between communist North Vietnam (supported by the Soviet Union and China) and non-communist South Vietnam (backed by the U.S. and allies).

6. <u>**Containment and the Truman Doctrine (1947)**</u> President Harry Truman articulated a policy of containment, aiming to prevent the spread of communism, and provided economic and military assistance to countries resisting communist influence, starting with Greece and Turkey.

7. <u>**Berlin Airlift (1948-1949)**</u> In response to Western efforts to unify Germany, the Soviet Union blockaded West Berlin. The U.S. and its allies organized the Berlin Airlift to supply the city with necessities, preventing a Soviet takeover.

8. <u>**Cuban Missile Crisis (1962)**</u> The discovery of Soviet missiles in Cuba led to a tense standoff between the U.S. and the Soviet Union, bringing the world to the brink of nuclear war. A resolution was reached through diplomatic means.

9. **<u>Détente</u>** In the 1970s, both superpowers pursued détente, a period of improved relations and reduced tensions, resulting in arms control agreements like the Strategic Arms Limitation Talks (SALT).

10. **<u>End of the Cold War</u>**

<u>Soviet Economic Decline</u> The Soviet Union faced economic decline and internal challenges, exacerbated by military expenditures.

<u>Reform Policies</u> Soviet leader Mikhail Gorbachev introduced reform policies (glasnost and perestroika) to address internal issues and improve relations with the West.

<u>Fall of the Berlin Wall (1989)</u> The symbolic collapse of the Berlin Wall marked the beginning of the end of the Cold War.

<u>Dissolution of the Soviet Union (1991)</u> The Soviet Union dissolved, leading to the emergence of independent states, and the Cold War officially came to an end.

The Cold War left a lasting impact on global geopolitics, shaping alliances, influencing conflicts, and defining the parameters of international relations for much of the 20th century. Its conclusion marked a new era characterized by changes in power dynamics, the emergence of new geopolitical challenges, and the reconfiguration of global alliances.

Chapter 22

<u>Post-WWII Decolonization</u>

Post-World War II decolonization refers to the process by which many European colonies gained independence in the aftermath of World War II. The war had profound effects on global power dynamics, economic structures, and ideologies, which, in turn, influenced the decolonization movement. Here's a detailed exploration of post-World War II decolonization.

1. **<u>Impact of World War II</u>**

<u>Weakened Colonial Powers</u> The war severely weakened European colonial powers economically and militarily.

<u>Changing Global Attitudes</u> The war exposed the hypocrisy of colonial powers fighting for freedom and democracy while suppressing the aspirations of colonized peoples.

2. **<u>Key Factors Driving Decolonization</u>**

<u>Nationalism</u> Colonized populations, inspired by the rhetoric of self-determination during the war, began demanding independence and sovereignty.

<u>Global Power Shifts</u> The decline of European powers and the rise of the United States and the Soviet Union as superpowers influenced the dynamics of decolonization.

<u>Economic Strain</u> Maintaining empires became economically unsustainable for many colonial powers, especially in the face of post-war reconstruction efforts.

3. **<u>India and Pakistan (1947)</u>**

<u>Indian Independence</u> India, one of the largest British colonies, gained independence in 1947 through a peaceful struggle led by Mahatma Gandhi and Jawaharlal Nehru.

<u>Partition</u> The creation of Pakistan as a separate state for Muslims resulted in the mass migration and communal violence.

4. **<u>Indochina and Vietnam (1954)</u>**

Geneva Accords The First Indochina War concluded with the Geneva Accords in 1954, leading to the temporary division of Vietnam along the 17th parallel.

Vietnam War The division set the stage for the Vietnam War, ultimately resulting in the reunification of North and South Vietnam in 1975.

5. African Decolonization (1950s-1960s)

Pan-Africanism The ideology of Pan-Africanism, promoting unity among African nations, gained momentum.

Gold Coast (Ghana) Kwame Nkrumah led Ghana to independence from British rule in 1957, becoming the first sub-Saharan African nation to gain independence.

6. Algerian War of Independence (1954-1962)

National Liberation Front (FLN) The Algerian National Liberation Front waged a war against French colonial rule.

Independence Algeria gained independence in 1962 after a prolonged and violent struggle.

7. Kenya (1963)

Mau Mau Uprising The Mau Mau Uprising in Kenya against British rule contributed to the country's eventual independence.

Independence Kenya gained independence in 1963.

8. Suez Crisis (1956)

Nationalization of the Suez Canal Egyptian President Gamal Abdel Nasser's nationalization of the Suez Canal prompted military intervention by Britain, France, and Israel.

International Pressure The United States and the Soviet Union opposed the intervention, marking a shift in global power dynamics and signaling the decline of traditional colonial powers.

9. Portuguese and Dutch Decolonization

Portuguese Colonial Wars Portugal's African colonies faced protracted wars of independence, with Mozambique, Angola, and Cape Verde gaining independence in the mid-1970s.

Indonesian Independence Indonesia gained independence from Dutch colonial rule in 1949 after a war of independence.

10. **Legacy and Challenges**

Legacy of Colonialism Decolonization did not erase the legacies of colonialism, as newly independent nations faced challenges such as economic dependency, political instability, and ethnic tensions.

Neocolonialism Some argue that the economic and political influence of former colonial powers persisted in the form of neocolonialism, impacting the sovereignty of newly independent nations.

Post-World War II decolonization was a transformative period that reshaped the global political landscape. The emergence of numerous independent nations in Asia, Africa, and the Middle East altered power dynamics, challenged traditional colonial structures, and contributed to the development of a more multi-polar world.

Chapter 23

<u>Civil Rights Movement</u>

The Civil Rights Movement was a social and political movement in the United States that aimed to end racial segregation and discrimination against African Americans and promote their constitutional rights and equal opportunities. The movement spanned the mid-1950s to the late 1960s and marked a crucial chapter in American history. Here's a detailed exploration of the Civil Rights Movement.

1. **<u>Background</u>**

<u>Jim Crow Era</u> The post-Reconstruction era in the late 19th and early 20th centuries saw the establishment of Jim Crow laws, enforcing racial segregation and institutionalizing discrimination against African Americans in the Southern United States.

<u>Plessy v. Ferguson (1896)</u> The Supreme Court decision in Plessy v. Ferguson upheld the "separate but equal" doctrine, allowing racial segregation in public facilities.

2. **<u>Brown v. Board of Education (1954)</u>**

<u>Landmark Supreme Court Decision</u> The Supreme Court's ruling in Brown v. Board of Education declared state laws establishing separate public schools for black and white students to be unconstitutional.

<u>End of Legal Segregation</u> The decision marked the beginning of the end of legal segregation and laid the groundwork for desegregation efforts.

3. **<u>Montgomery Bus Boycott (1955-1956)</u>**

<u>Rosa Parks</u> Rosa Parks, an African American woman, refused to give up her bus seat to a white person in Montgomery, Alabama, sparking the Montgomery Bus Boycott.

<u>Leadership of Martin Luther King Jr.</u> The boycott, led by Martin Luther King Jr., was a successful protest against segregated seating on city buses.

4. **Southern Christian Leadership Conference (SCLC)** Martin Luther King Jr., along with other leaders, founded the SCLC in 1957 as a nonviolent organization to coordinate and support the Civil Rights Movement.

5. **Sit-Ins and Freedom Rides**

Student Activism In the early 1960s, college students initiated sit-ins at segregated lunch counters and participated in Freedom Rides, challenging segregation on interstate buses.

Integration Success These efforts contributed to the desegregation of public facilities.

6. **March on Washington (1963)**

Mass Protest The March on Washington for Jobs and Freedom in 1963 attracted hundreds of thousands of participants and culminated in Martin Luther King Jr.'s iconic "I Have a Dream" speech.

Civil Rights Act of 1964 The march contributed to the passage of the Civil Rights Act of 1964, which outlawed discrimination based on race, color, religion, sex, or national origin.

7. **Voting Rights Act of 1965**

Voting Barriers African Americans faced significant barriers to voting, including literacy tests and poll taxes.

Selma to Montgomery March The Selma to Montgomery marches in 1965 brought attention to voting rights issues and contributed to the passage of the Voting Rights Act, which aimed to eliminate discriminatory voting practices.

8. **Black Power Movement**

Emergence The Black Power movement, which gained prominence in the mid-1960s, emphasized racial pride, self-determination, and solidarity.

Leadership Figures like Malcolm X and organizations like the Black Panther Party played key roles in the movement.

9. **Fair Housing Act of 1968** The Fair Housing Act aimed to address racial discrimination in housing by prohibiting discrimination in the sale, rental, and financing of housing.

10. **Legacy and Continued Struggle**

Legal Changes The Civil Rights Movement led to significant legal changes, challenging discriminatory laws and practices.

Continued Challenges Despite legal advancements, challenges related to systemic racism, economic inequality, and social justice persist, leading to ongoing discussions and activism.

The Civil Rights Movement marked a transformative period in American history, challenging entrenched racial inequalities and inspiring subsequent movements for social justice. Its impact extended beyond legal changes, influencing public attitudes and fostering a broader awareness of the ongoing struggle for civil rights and equality.

Chapter 24

<u>Space Race</u>

The Space Race was a period of intense competition and exploration between the United States and the Soviet Union during the Cold War, primarily from the late 1950s to the early 1970s. It was characterized by a series of milestones in space exploration, with each superpower striving to achieve significant technological and scientific accomplishments. Here's a detailed exploration of the Space Race.

1. **<u>Origins</u>**

<u>Post-World War II Developments</u> After World War II, both the United States and the Soviet Union sought to capitalize on German rocket technology and scientific expertise.

<u>Geopolitical Tensions</u> The ideological and geopolitical rivalry between the United States and the Soviet Union during the Cold War contributed to the space competition.

2. **<u>Sputnik 1 (1957)</u>**

<u>First Artificial Satellite</u> The Soviet Union launched Sputnik 1 on October 4, 1957, marking the first artificial satellite in orbit around Earth.

<u>Impact</u> Sputnik's success had a profound impact, creating a sense of urgency and concern in the United States and leading to increased funding for space exploration.

3. **<u>Yuri Gagarin (1961)</u>**

<u>First Human in Space</u> On April 12, 1961, Soviet cosmonaut Yuri Gagarin became the first human to orbit Earth aboard the spacecraft Vostok 1.

<u>Symbolic Victory</u> Gagarin's achievement was a symbolic victory for the Soviet Union, showcasing its technological prowess.

4. **<u>Mercury and Gemini Programs (United States)</u>**

Project Mercury The United States responded with Project Mercury, which aimed to put Americans into space. Alan Shepard became the first American in space in 1961.

Project Gemini The Gemini program (1961-1966) focused on developing the skills needed for future Apollo moon missions, including spacewalks and orbital maneuvers.

5. **Apollo Program (United States)**

Apollo 11 (1969) On July 20, 1969, NASA's Apollo 11 mission successfully landed astronauts Neil Armstrong and Buzz Aldrin on the Moon. Armstrong's famous words, "That's one small step for [a] man, one giant leap for mankind," marked a historic achievement.

Subsequent Missions The Apollo program continued with several successful missions, including Apollo 12, Apollo 14, Apollo 15, Apollo 16, and Apollo 17.

6. **Lunar Missions (Soviet Union)**

Lunar Probes While the Soviet Union achieved significant milestones in space, including the first human in space, their efforts to land humans on the Moon were not successful.

Luna Program The Luna program involved a series of robotic missions, with Luna 2 becoming the first human-made object to reach the Moon in 1959.

7. **Space Race Achievements**

Spacewalks Both the United States and the Soviet Union achieved spacewalks, with Alexei Leonov (USSR) becoming the first person to conduct a spacewalk in 1965, and Ed White (United States) performs the first American spacewalk in 1965.

Space Stations The Soviet Union launched the first space station, Salyut 1, in 1971. The United States later established Skylab in 1973.

8. **International Cooperation – Apollo-Soyuz Test Project (1972)** The United States and the Soviet Union conducted the Apollo-Soyuz Test Project, a joint space mission symbolizing the end of the Space Race and the beginning of international cooperation in space.

9. **Legacy**

Technological Advancements The Space Race led to significant technological advancements, including the development of rocketry, satellite technology, and computer systems.

Scientific Discoveries The exploration of space provided valuable scientific data about Earth, the Moon, and the broader universe.

10. **Modern Space Exploration**

International Space Station (ISS) The ISS, established in the 1990s, represents a collaborative effort involving multiple countries in space research and exploration.

Mars Exploration Ongoing efforts include robotic missions to Mars and plans for human exploration of the red planet.

The Space Race was a defining chapter in the history of space exploration, driven by geopolitical competition and the desire to push the boundaries of human achievement. While it had its roots in Cold War tensions, it laid the foundation for continued exploration and collaboration in space.

Chapter 25

<u>Contemporary Era</u>

The Contemporary Era refers to the current historical period, typically considered to begin in the late 20th century and extend to the present day. It is characterized by significant global changes, technological advancements, political shifts, and cultural transformations. Here's a detailed exploration of the Contemporary Era.

1. **<u>End of the Cold War (1989-1991)</u>**

<u>Fall of the Berlin Wall</u> The Berlin Wall fell in 1989, symbolizing the end of the division between East and West Germany and the beginning of the end of the Cold War.

<u>Dissolution of the Soviet Union</u> The Soviet Union dissolved in 1991, leading to the emergence of independent states and marking the end of bipolar superpower competition.

2. **<u>Globalization</u>**

<u>Economic Integration</u> The Contemporary Era is marked by increased economic interconnectedness and globalization, facilitated by advancements in technology, communication, and transportation.

<u>Multinational Corporations</u> Multinational corporations play a significant role in global trade, investment, and production.

3. **<u>Information Age and Technology</u>**

<u>Digital Revolution</u> The rapid development of digital technologies, including the internet and mobile communication, has transformed the way information is accessed, shared, and communicated.

<u>Tech Giants</u> Companies like Apple, Google, Microsoft, and Facebook have become global giants, shaping the digital landscape.

4. **<u>War on Terror (2001-present)</u>**

<u>September 11 Attacks</u> The terrorist attacks on September 11, 2001, led to a global response and the initiation of the War on Terror by the United States.

War in Afghanistan The U.S. and its allies engaged in military operations in Afghanistan, targeting the Taliban and Al-Qaeda.

Iraq War The invasion of Iraq in 2003, based on the belief of weapons of mass destruction, led to significant geopolitical consequences and ongoing conflicts.

5. **Rise of China**

Economic Growth China's rapid economic growth has positioned it as a major global player, impacting international trade, politics, and technology.

Belt and Road Initiative China's Belt and Road Initiative aims to enhance global infrastructure and connectivity.

6. **Climate Change and Environmental Concerns**

Global Environmental Challenges The Contemporary Era has witnessed increased awareness of environmental issues, including climate change, deforestation, and pollution.

International Agreements Efforts such as the Paris Agreement aim to address climate change through global cooperation.

7. **Human Rights and Social Movements**

Advancements in Human Rights The Contemporary Era has seen progress in recognizing and advocating for human rights, including LGBTQ+ rights, gender equality, and racial justice.

Social Movements Movements such as Black Lives Matter, Me Too, and climate activism have gained prominence, advocating for social change and justice.

8. **Health Challenges**

Pandemics The world has faced significant health challenges, including the HIV/AIDS pandemic, the H1N1 influenza pandemic, and the global response to the COVID-19 pandemic.

Medical Advances Advances in medical research and technology have contributed to improved healthcare and vaccinations.

9. <u>**Political Changes**</u>

<u>**Shifts in Global Power**</u> The Contemporary Era has seen shifts in global power dynamics, with the rise of new players and changes in political alliances.

<u>**Populism**</u> The rise of populist movements in various countries has influenced political landscapes and policies.

10. <u>**Social Media and Communication**</u>

<u>**Social Media Impact**</u> Platforms like Facebook, Twitter, and Instagram have transformed communication, activism, and information dissemination.

<u>**Fake News and Misinformation**</u> The ease of sharing information online has led to challenges related to misinformation and the spread of fake news.

The Contemporary Era is a dynamic and rapidly changing period marked by complex challenges and opportunities. It is characterized by the ongoing interplay of political, economic, technological, and social forces that shape the trajectory of the world in the 21st century.